SCIENCE DISCOVERY

Health

Q&A

Celeste A. Peters

www.av2books.com

AV² provides enriched content that supplements and complements this book. Weigl's AV² books strive to create inspired learning and engage young minds in a total learning experience.

Your AV² Media Enhanced books come alive with...

 Audio
Listen to sections of the book read aloud.

 Key Words
Study vocabulary, and complete a matching word activity.

 Video
Watch informative video clips.

 Quizzes
Test your knowledge.

Go to **www.av2books.com**, and enter this book's unique code.

BOOK CODE

E772200

 Embedded Weblinks
Gain additional information for research.

 Slide Show
View images and captions, and prepare a presentation.

AV² by Weigl brings you media enhanced books that support active learning.

 Try This!
Complete activities and hands-on experiments.

... and much, much more!

Published by AV² by Weigl
350 5th Avenue, 59th Floor
New York, NY 10118
Website: www.av2books.com   www.weigl.com

Library of Congress Cataloging-in-Publication Data
Peters, Celeste A. (Celeste Andra), 1953-
[Health]
Health Q & A / Celeste A. Peters.
    p. cm. -- (Science discovery)
Originally published as Health. New York : Weigl Publishers, 2009.
Includes bibliographical references and index.
Audience: 4-6.
ISBN 978-1-62127-414-8 (hardcover : alk. paper) -- ISBN 978-1-62127-420-9 (pbk. : alk. paper)
1. Health--Juvenile literature. 2. Exercise--Juvenile literature. 3. Children's questions and answers. I. Title. II. Title: Health questions & answers. III. Title: Health questions and answers.
RA777.P48 2013
613--dc23
                    2012039657

Printed in the United States of America, in North Mankato, Minnesota
1 2 3 4 5 6 7 8 9 0 17 16 15 14 13

062013
WEP040413B

Project coordinator Aaron Carr   Designer Mandy Christiansen

Every reasonable effort has been made to trace ownership and to obtain permission to reprint copyright material. The publishers would be pleased to have any errors or omissions brought to their attention so that they may be corrected in subsequent printings.

Photo Credits
Weigl acknowledges Getty Images as its primary image supplier for this title.

Contents

What Is Good Health?

Many people have wondered what it means to be healthy, why people sometimes get sick, or how doctors can treat certain illnesses. How people feel has a big impact on their lives. It is easy for people to run laps around the schoolyard when they are feeling well. However, if they try doing the same thing when they have an upset stomach, they may not make it far. People need to be healthy to do their best.

The human body has amazing ways to fight illness and disease while remaining in top shape, but people must take care of it. The ancient Greeks believed that good health meant having both a fit body and a fit mind. The brain works better if the body is in good shape. The body suffers fewer aches and pains if the mind is free of stress. Personal cleanliness, regular exercise, and eating healthful foods are keys to good health.

How Do Scientists Use Inquiry to Answer Questions?

When scientists try to answer a question, they follow the process of scientific inquiry. They begin by making observations and asking questions. Then, they propose an answer to their question. This is called the hypothesis. The hypothesis guides scientists as they research the issue. Research can involve performing experiments or reading books on the subject. When their research is finished, scientists examine their results and review their hypothesis. Often, they discover that their hypothesis was incorrect. If this happens, they revise their hypothesis and go through the process of scientific inquiry again.

Process of Scientific Inquiry

Observation

Being healthy is important. There are factors involved in being able to support good health. So what is good health?

Have You Answered the Question?

The cycle of scientific inquiry never truly ends. For example, once scientists and doctors know how much sleep an adult might need to stay healthy, they might ask, "How much sleep does a child or adolescent need to stay healthy? Are there differences in sleep requirements for older or younger people?"

Research

Scientists and doctors have identified sleep, exercise, and a good diet, as important aspects of a healthful lifestyle. They have done this by asking questions, such as, "What foods are best for healthful living?" and "How much sleep do people need to stay healthy?"

Hypothesis

Scientists try to answer these questions by stating a hypothesis. For example, a hypothesis might be that people need eight hours of sleep every night to maintain a healthful lifestyle.

Results

Results of an experiment or test are reviewed and checked for accuracy. The results are compared to the hypothesis. Do the results support the hypothesis? If not, a new experiment or test may be needed.

Experiment

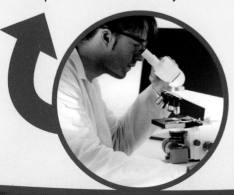

To answer a hypothesis, tests or experiments are done to find answers. Perhaps, with sleep, people are asked questions to find out how much sleep they get in a normal night and whether or not they have enough energy throughout the day.

Why Is It Important to Have a Healthful Diet?

People can starve to death if they do not eat. However, health is much more than eating enough food to survive. It is important for people to eat healthful food. The key to a healthful diet is eating a variety of healthful foods, such as fresh fruits and vegetables. Such foods contain **nutrients,** such as **vitamins** and **minerals**. Vitamins and minerals do not supply energy, but they are needed for the body to work properly.

A varied diet is important because not all foods contain the same nutrients. Imagine if someone only ate oranges. This person would get plenty of vitamin C but none of the mineral **calcium**. If a person eats only fish, he or she would have a great deal of vitamin A but no vitamin C. The human body needs a balance of different vitamins and minerals to function properly.

Certain vitamins and minerals are so important that a person can become very sick if he or she does not eat enough of them. Before this was known, sailors at sea went for long periods without eating fresh fruits and vegetables. As a result, they often became sick and died from a disease called scurvy. Scurvy is caused by the lack of vitamin C. Vitamin C is found in many fruits and vegetables, especially citrus fruits, such as oranges and grapefruit.

❯ Many doctors recommend a diet high in fresh fruits and vegetables.

Digging Deeper

Your Challenge!

Try this experiment to see how salt affects your body. Have an adult cut a potato in half. Fill two small bowls with water, and mix two tablespoons of salt into one of the bowls. Then, place each potato part in the water with the cut side down. Wait 30 minutes. What happened to the potato in the salty water? The salt pulled the water out of the potato. This is why salty foods and drinks make people thirsty.

Summary

Eating a balanced diet is important to good health. Having a diet of fresh fruits and vegetables is especially important because you can get the vitamins, minerals, and other nutrients you need to be healthy.

Further Inquiry

Eating well is important for good health. It supplies the body with energy for exercise. Maybe we should ask,

What can exercise do for health?

What Can Exercise Do for Health?

Regular exercise improves a person's posture, works off mental stress, and helps a person sleep well at night. Best of all, regular exercise helps keep people fit. This is important because a fit body works best.

Several changes take place in the body when a person exercises regularly. Muscles and bones grow stronger. The heart becomes a better pump. The lungs work more efficiently, which means that they can deliver more oxygen to the body. The body relies on oxygen to turn the food a person eats into the energy muscles need to function.

Muscles work as the body's motor, keeping it moving during exercise. In order to grow, however, muscles also need rest and protein. Protein is found in foods such as meat, fish, eggs, dairy products, beans, and legumes. The body needs protein to build muscle, heal wounds, and fight infection. If muscles do not get enough rest and protein, they will not grow, no matter how hard a person exercises.

▲ Muscles use more energy when they are exercised. They also use more oxygen.

Digging Deeper

Your Challenge!

How do your muscles get more oxygen? Find out by completing this challenge.

1. Take your pulse. Write down how many times your heart beats in one minute.

2. Run in place or do some other fast exercise for two minutes.

3. Repeat the first step.

You will find out that exercise increases your heart rate.

Summary

Exercise is an important part of keeping healthy.

Further Inquiry

Exercise is good for the body. Sometimes, too much exercise, or the wrong type of exercise, causes painful injuries. Maybe we should ask,

What is pain?

What Is Pain?

Nobody likes to be in pain. People try to avoid being in pain by staying healthy and safe, but sometimes, it cannot be avoided. Believe it or not, people need pain. It can save a person's life.

Pain is the body's warning system. It sends a message loud and clear when something is wrong. Imagine what it would be like if people could not sense pain. If they cut themselves, they could bleed to death without realizing they were hurt. If their clothes caught on fire, they might not know before they were seriously burned.

When something damages the body, the **cells** in the injured area send out chemicals. These chemicals activate nearby nerves, the fibers that send messages between the brain and the rest of the body. These nerves send an urgent message to the brain. Almost instantly, the person feels pain in the injured area. At the same time, the brain sends a return message to the affected area that says, "Get out of there." If the pain is caused by an outside force, such as heat from the burner on a stove, the person will immediately pull away from whatever is hurting them.

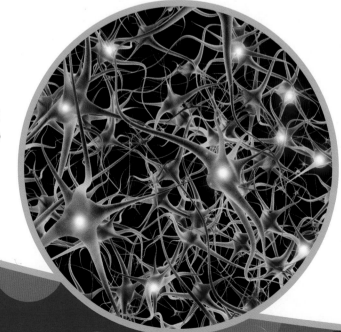

> Information about pain travels through the body as an electrical or chemical signal. This signal travels to the brain through special cells called neurons.

Digging Deeper

Your Challenge!

Pain helps your body protect itself. If you get hurt, your body will go on to fix itself. Research online and in a library to find out what steps the body takes to heal itself of a broken bone. Create a chart of these steps, from the first pain to the healed bone.

Summary

Pain is part of the body's system for keeping healthy and safe. Pain tells our brain that we need to do something, such as move our hand from a hot flame.

Further Inquiry

Pain can come from injury or from not resting the body enough. Maybe we should ask,

What else is needed for a healthy body?

∧ Some kinds of injuries can be treated with ice and rest.

What Else Is Needed for a Healthy Body?

Many things are needed for a healthy body, but one of the most important is sleep. When a person does not get enough sleep for several nights in a row, they may become sick. There is a good reason why this happens. The **immune system** becomes more active while a person sleeps. It goes into high gear, fighting off **germs** that have invaded the body.

If a person does not sleep long enough, the immune system does not have a chance to do its job. The germs may win the battle. Sleep gives the body and mind a chance to rest. Well-rested muscles recover more quickly from exercise and grow stronger. Not getting enough sleep can cause the brain to work slowly. This will affect learning and behavior.

About eight to twelve hours of sleep per night is best for children. Adults need seven to eight hours of sleep. Newborn babies sleep an average of 16 to 18 hours per day. Teenagers need about nine hours of sleep every night. Older adults need as much sleep as younger adults, but they tend to sleep less at night. Elderly people are more likely to suffer from sleep disorders, such as insomnia. People with insomnia have trouble falling asleep or staying asleep.

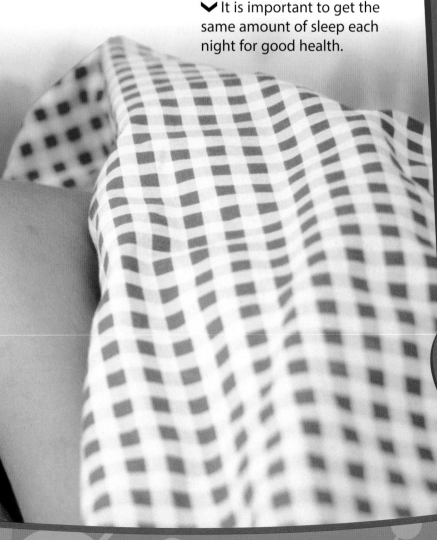

⌄ It is important to get the same amount of sleep each night for good health.

Digging Deeper

Your Challenge!

Calculate how much sleep you are getting on a normal night. Write down the time you go to bed and the time you wake up. How many total hours are you sleeping? Do you need more sleep?

Summary

Sleep is important for staying healthy. Getting the right amount of sleep each night will help our bodies function better. Not getting enough sleep may make us sick, since the immune system cannot work as well when we are tired.

Further Inquiry

Sleep is important to good health. Not getting enough can make us feel ill. Germs can also make us sick. We might ask,

How does the body defend against germs?

How Does the Body Defend Against Germs?

Millions of germs try to invade the body every day. People cannot normally see germs, but they are in the air people breathe and on the food they eat.

The body's biggest defense against germs is skin. The only way germs can get past skin is through cuts and scratches, and through openings such as the nose or mouth. The body has other defenses to stop germs that get through the skin.

The nose and mouth trap germs with a sticky substance called mucus. Ears have wax in them to trap germs. Tears in the eyes wash germs out and contain a chemical that kills bacteria. If germs get past all these defenses, they face the immune system. White blood cells called phagocytes and lymphocytes are the immune system's most powerful weapons. These cells attack any germs that get into the body.

Phagocytes flow through the blood and "eat" germs. Lymphocytes launch an "army" of antibodies. Each antibody kills a different type of germ. It covers the germ in a substance that attracts phagocytes. The body remembers how to make the antibody for each type of germ. If the same type of germ comes back, the body can fight it off easily. This protection from disease is called immunity.

❯ Germs are microscopic and cannot be seen without magnification.

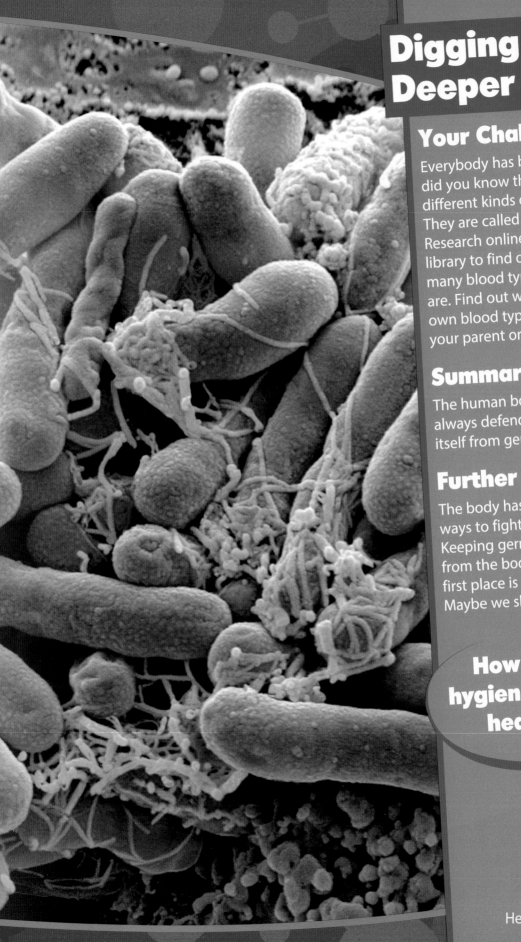

Digging Deeper

Your Challenge!

Everybody has blood, but did you know that there different kinds of blood? They are called blood types. Research online and in a library to find out how many blood types there are. Find out what your own blood type is from your parent or guardian.

Summary

The human body is always defending itself from germs.

Further Inquiry

The body has many ways to fight off germs. Keeping germs away from the body in the first place is a good idea. Maybe we should ask,

How does hygiene affect health?

How Does Hygiene Affect Health?

Hygiene means staying healthy by having a clean body. Germs are washed away when people shower or bathe, or when they wash their hands. Washing regularly, especially after a person sweats, is part of keeping healthy.

When a person does not wash or bathe, they can get sore, red pimples on their body, especially on their face, neck, or back. This is called acne. Acne is caused by a natural oil produced by the skin. This oil mixes with sweat and dead skin to form an oily layer on the skin. Germs invade this layer and cause acne to flare up. Washing with soap and warm water a few times each day helps to keep the oily layer from building up.

It is also important for people to keep their teeth clean. A type of bacteria called plaque is to blame for cavities and bad breath. Plaque lives on teeth and uses the sugars left behind after a person eats. Plaque also makes an acid that can eat right through tooth enamel, the hard substance that covers teeth. Brushing and flossing help keep plaque under control.

❯ Regular hand washing helps prevent the spread of germs.

Sweat and oils can build up on the skin after exercise. Most athletes shower after a game or practice.

Your Challenge!

Germs, bacteria, and even fungi exist all around us, even on the foods we eat. Try this experiment to see how a fungus grows. Use a cotton swab to collect some dust. Place the swab on a piece of bread. Put five drops of water on the bread, and seal the bread in a plastic sandwich bag. Leave the bread in the bag for a week and record your results.

Summary

Good hygiene means keeping the body clean. Hygiene is important to health.

Further Inquiry

Good hygiene fights off germs, keeping the body in balance, or **homeostasis**. Maybe we should ask,

How does homeostasis protect the body?

How Does Homeostasis Protect the Body?

In order for a person to stay healthy, the **environment** in their body should always remain the same. The body's temperature must stay close to 98.6° Fahrenheit (37° Celsius). The amount of blood and other fluids must not suddenly increase or decrease too much.

Homeostasis is the process that keeps the environment inside the body the same when possible. Imagine it is a freezing-cold day. A person has been outside snowboarding for the afternoon. His hands, feet, and face are cold. Why? Homeostasis is at work protecting the person. All the warm blood is flowing around important organs such as the heart and lungs. In addition, homeostasis might make muscles twitch or shiver. This creates heat, so the body can stay at the right temperature.

Homeostasis also protects people when they go outside on a very hot day. It cools them down by activating **glands** that make people sweat. The sweat cools the skin to keep people from getting too hot. However, homeostasis may sometimes make a person's temperature rise. When a person has a fever, the heat helps the body destroy the germs that are making the person ill.

❯ Wearing the correct type of clothing can help protect the body from extreme temperatures.

Digging Deeper

Your Challenge!

Create a cause and effect chart. Write down 10 different situations that affect your body, such as cold weather, hot weather, sleeping, or exercising. These are the causes. Next to each cause, write an effect this situation has on your body. Finally, write down how your body reacts to each cause in order to maintain homeostasis.

Summary

Homeostasis is the process that keeps the environment inside the body mostly the same when possible. This keeps people healthy.

Further Inquiry

Despite the body's defenses, people still get sick. Maybe we should ask,

How does disease spread?

⌃ Hot weather can quickly upset homeostasis. It is important to try and stay cool and drink water in hot weather.

Q&A

How Does Disease Spread?

Diseases are caused by germs. When germs get past all of a person's defenses, they make that person sick. Many diseases can be passed between people. These diseases are **contagious**.

Many objects have germs on them. People should wash their hands frequently to avoid getting sick. Imagine a group of people is in an elevator. Someone sneezes without covering their mouth. Millions of germs fly out into the air—the same air everyone else is breathing. Some people wear masks when they are ill. This keeps germs from spreading.

Surgeons wear masks in the operating room so that germs in their breath will not infect their patients. Germs can get into food and water. This gives them direct contact with the stomach. There are several ways a person can protect against these germs. Wash raw fruits and vegetables thoroughly before eating them. Eat only well-cooked meat. Boil untreated water before using it. Most water in the United States and Canada is treated, which means that harmful bacteria, germs, and unpleasant tastes and smells have been removed.

❯ Germs released from a sneeze travel at about 100 miles (160 kilometers) per hour.

Digging Deeper

Your Challenge!

In the 1300s, a disease called the bubonic plague spread through Europe. It entered humans through fleas. This disease killed about 25 million people. Research online and in a library to create a timeline of the spread of this disease. Trace its spread from country to country. How long did it take to spread? Where did it start? When did it end?

Summary

Diseases are caused by germs and can spread many different ways. It is important to practice good hygiene and follow tips for living healthy.

Further Inquiry

Since their immune systems are still developing, children often get sick more often than adults. Maybe we should ask:

What are common childhood diseases?

❯ Surgeons use sterile tools during surgery to avoid bringing germs into a patient's body.

What Are Common Childhood Diseases?

There are several diseases that children are especially vulnerable to. These diseases include chicken pox, mumps, and measles. Chicken pox begins as a rash. The rash turns into clear, fluid-filled bumps. The bumps itch and form scabs. It is not good to scratch the bumps. Germs from fingers can infect the bumps and leave scars. Chicken pox can cause fever, tiredness, or loss of appetite. In rare cases, it can even be fatal. Symptoms of measles include fever and a rash. Mumps causes a child's face to swell. Both of these diseases can be dangerous if not treated.

Thanks to advancements in medicine, many childhood diseases are not as common as they used to be in the United States. Children are usually given **vaccines** that make them immune to diseases such as chicken pox, mumps, and measles. Elsewhere in the world, often in under-developed countries, these diseases are still a problem. Through advancements in medicine, fewer people will suffer from disease.

A high temperature is usually a sign that the body is infected.

Your Challenge!

Polio is a disease that affected millions of people in the past and still affects people today. In 1955, a doctor named Jonas Salk introduced a vaccine for polio. Research online and in a library to create a graph that shows the number of polio cases in the United States from 1900 to 2000. How did Salk's vaccine affect the number of polio cases in this period?

Summary

Chicken pox, mumps, and measles are common childhood diseases. Most children in the United States receive vaccines to prevent them from getting these diseases. However, such vaccines are not available worldwide.

Further Inquiry

Some people have **allergies** to some medicines. Maybe we should ask,

What causes allergies?

What Causes Allergies?

Millions of people in North America have allergies. Allergies occur when a person's immune system overreacts to substances that are usually harmless, such as dust or certain foods. Substances that cause allergies are called allergens.

When the immune system mistakes something, such as a peanut, for an invader, it tries to destroy it. As part of its response, the immune system releases chemicals, such as histamine. These chemicals trigger the symptoms, or signs, of an allergy. The allergy symptoms a person experiences depend on where the chemicals are released in the body. When the chemicals are released in the eyes and nose, they cause sneezing, runny nose, and itchy eyes. When they are released in the stomach, they cause diarrhea and vomiting. When they are released in the skin, they cause swelling, redness, and hives.

If the chemicals are released in the lungs, they cause swelling in the respiratory system. The chemicals can create a great deal of mucus. This can trigger an **asthma** attack. People with asthma are often allergic to plant pollen, molds, or certain foods. Allergens are not the only triggers. Exercise, smoke, cold air, perfume, aspirin, and food additives can cause an asthma attack. An asthma attack makes it difficult to breathe. People who suffer from asthma carry special medicine with them in case they have an asthma attack.

❯ Many people suffer from seasonal allergies in the spring or fall.

Digging Deeper

Your Challenge!

Research why some allergies are especially harmful. Use the library and the Internet and research a dangerous allergy, such as bee stings. Find out why this allergy is so serious. Do you know anyone with this allergy? If so, interview that person to find out more about it.

Summary

Allergies cause the immune system to overreact to substances that are often harmless. Allergies can be dangerous if careful attention is not given to avoiding those substances.

Further Inquiry

Sometimes, the immune system is unable to fight off a disease. Doctors then will use medicines to help the body. Maybe we should ask,

How do medicines work?

How Do Medicines Work?

Your immune system is very good at fighting germs. Sometimes, it cannot do the job on its own and it needs help. Antibiotics are medicines that weaken and kill bacteria. Antibiotics are like poisons that are designed to attack a specific bacteria and nothing else. There are different antibiotics for different kinds of infections.

It is important for people to finish all the antibiotics the doctor prescribes, even if they begin to feel better. If a person stops taking them too soon, some bacteria will remain in the body. These will multiply and make the person sick again.

Analgesics are a type of painkiller. There are two types of analgesics. An anti-inflammatory analgesic, such as aspirin, dissolves in the stomach and enters the bloodstream. Once in the bloodstream, the analgesic moves throughout the body, stopping any other chemicals that are telling the brain to sense pain. An opioid analgesic, such as morphine, is much stronger. It goes straight to the **spinal cord** and brain to block pain messages. Anesthetics are medications used during surgery that are stronger than opioids. They make it very difficult for one nerve cell to send messages to the next. Pain signals never reach the brain, and the person falls into a deep sleep.

❯ Viruses and bacteria are not the same, though both can make a person sick. Antibiotics do not work on viruses.

Digging Deeper

Your Challenge!

Work with an adult or guardian to take inventory of the different medicines in your home. Find out what these medicines treat and who you should go to if you ever need to take medicine.

Summary

Medicines help people when they are sick. There are different types of medicines.

Further Inquiry

Some diseases cannot be cured with medicine yet. Diabetes is one such disease. It affects many people. Maybe we should ask,

Why do diabetics need insulin?

Why Do Diabetics Need Insulin?

Diabetes is a disease that occurs when the body has problems producing or using insulin. Insulin is a chemical that helps sugar enter the cells of the body. Cells need sugar because it provides the energy that they need to work. Without insulin to help process sugar, cells starve, and sugar builds up in the blood.

Insulin is produced by an organ called the pancreas. Some people have a pancreas that cannot make enough insulin.
They have a disease called Type I diabetes. They must take daily insulin shots and follow a special diet.

❯ Most people with diabetes measure their blood sugar daily to find out their blood sugar levels. This can be done at home using a touch monitor.

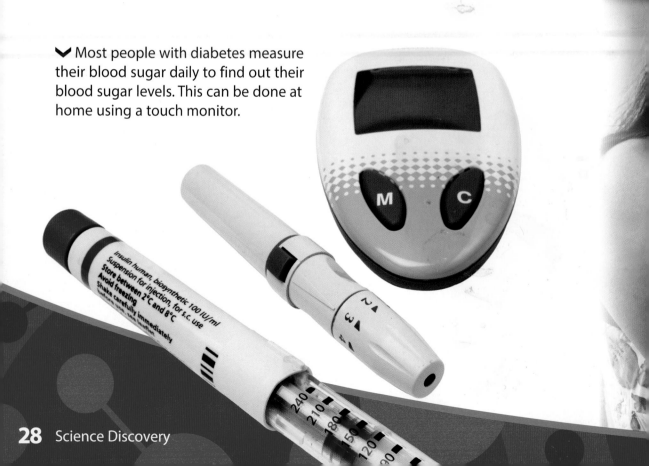

Most diabetics have Type II diabetes, and their pancreas creates enough insulin. However, their body is unable to make the insulin work as it should. These people can usually treat diabetes with exercise and a special diet. A few must take insulin injections. Untreated, diabetes can cause heart disease, stroke, kidney disease, blindness, nerve damage, and difficulty fighting off infections.

▼ In 2011, the American Diabetes Association reported that 25.8 million Americans have diabetes. More than 215,000 are children.

Digging Deeper

Your Challenge!

Too much sugar can harm your body. For one week, keep track of the sugar in everything you eat. Research online and in a library to find out how much sugar is in the foods you eat. Use measuring spoons to put the same amount of sugar in a jar. At the end of the week, check the jar to see how much sugar you ate in that time.

Summary

Diabetes is an illness that impacts many people. There are two forms: Type I and Type II. Treatments include insulin shots, changes in diet, and exercise.

Further Inquiry

Sometimes, the human body turns against itself, causing other diseases. These are called autoimmune diseases. Maybe we should ask,

What are autoimmune diseases?

What Are Autoimmune Diseases?

The human body is like a very complex computer. It is made up of many parts that perform different functions to keep the body healthy. Certain parts can break down, which can cause serious problems for the body.

Sometimes, the body's immune system makes a huge mistake. It begins attacking perfectly good body tissue. No one knows why it does this. The immune system simply considers this tissue an invader. This results in autoimmune diseases.

Rheumatoid **arthritis** is one of the most common autoimmune diseases. It begins some time between childhood and middle age. The immune system suddenly begins attacking body tissue in joints. Rheumatoid arthritis causes swelling and pain in joints and elsewhere in the body.

There are several other autoimmune diseases. Lupus attacks tissues in the skin, blood vessels, heart, and kidneys. Multiple sclerosis attacks the nerves. Some scientists now believe that Type I diabetes is caused by an autoimmune disease that attacks insulin-making cells in the pancreas.

❯ Rheumatoid arthritis can affect the joints in the hands.

▼ People with arthritis sometimes have trouble moving around.

Digging Deeper

Your Challenge!

Autoimmune disease rates vary for the type of disease. Research different autoimmune diseases and their symptoms. Then, create a bar graph showing the number of people in the United States who are affected by such diseases.

Summary

Autoimmune diseases occur when the body's immune system is not functioning properly and the body attacks its own tissue. Rheumatoid arthritis is an example.

Further Inquiry

Autoimmune diseases affect millions of people. Heart disease, however, affects even more. Maybe we should ask,

How does heart disease develop?

Q&A

How Does Heart Disease Develop?

Some people eat potato chips, hamburgers, fried chicken, pizza, and ice cream on a regular basis. These foods might appeal to their taste buds. However, such foods could be harming their hearts.

Heart disease is a condition that prevents the heart from working properly. The heart is a special type of muscle that pumps blood to other muscles and organs throughout the body. The left side of the heart pumps blood to the lungs, where it becomes **oxygenated**. Then, the oxygenated blood travels to right side of the heart. From there, it is pumped through **arteries** to the rest of the body. Special arteries, called coronary arteries, bring oxygenated blood to the heart itself. If a coronary artery becomes blocked, the heart does not receive the oxygen it needs to work. The result is a **heart attack**.

Plaque is the main cause of blocked arteries. This is not the same plaque that builds up on teeth. This plaque is quite different. It is a fatty substance that builds up on the insides of arteries. As it builds up, it leaves less and less room for blood to flow through.

There are two things a person can do to help prevent the buildup of plaque—exercise and limit the amount of saturated fats eaten. Saturated fats are found in foods such as red meat, poultry, dairy products, fried foods, coconut oil, and palm oil.

⌄ An unhealthful diet is one of the leading causes of heart disease in North America.

Digging Deeper

Your Challenge!

Heart disease can be prevented. Exercises, such as running and bicycle riding, help keep the heart strong. For this challenge, try to ride a bike for a total of one hour each day. Break up the ride throughout the day if you have to. As your heart becomes stronger, you will notice that riding for one hour is easier to do. Continue this challenge by riding for longer periods of time or by increasing your riding speed.

Summary

Heart disease is a serious problem in the United States. It can be partially avoided through exercise and eating healthful foods.

Further Inquiry

Heart disease is the leading cause of death in the U.S. A disease called cancer is second. Maybe we should ask,

What is cancer?

What Is Cancer?

Each year, many people in the United States find out that they have cancer. Although cancer can affect people at any age, it is more common in older adults. Each year in the United States, more than 500,000 people die of cancer.

Cancer is a disease that affects the cells of the body. A human begins as a single cell, the basic building block of most living material. This cell grows and splits into two separate cells. These cells divide and become four cells, then eight cells, then sixteen, and so on. This rapid multiplication continues until there are the trillions of cells that make up an adult body. Then, the process slows down.

The cells of an adult normally divide only when new cells are needed to replace old ones. Sometimes, a cell grows and multiplies out of control. All of the extra cells it creates clump together in a lump called a tumor. Many tumors are benign. This means they do not spread to other parts of the body. However, some tumors are malignant, or cancerous, and destroy the normal cells around them. If cancer cells break away from the tumor, they can form tumors in other parts of the body. This is how cancer spreads. When cancer spreads, it may begin to affect the proper working of other tissues and organs in the body. It may eventually cause death.

> ❯ Leukemia is a type of cancer that affects the blood. Doctors do not know what causes leukemia.

Digging Deeper

Your Challenge!

Many families in the United States have been affected by cancer. Ask a parent or guardian if your family has been affected by this disease. Now, take the challenge and volunteer your time to one of the many walking or running events that support cancer research.

Summary

Cancer involves cells that grow rapidly, out-of-control. Cancer can spread, even if diagnosed and treated. Many people suffer from cancer.

Further Inquiry

Smoking and drinking alcohol increases the risk of developing cancer. Maybe we should ask,

How do cigarettes and alcohol harm the body?

How Do Cigarettes and Alcohol Harm the Body?

Many people smoke or drink alcohol. Although they cannot see the effects inside their bodies, these things have very negative effects on their health. Cigarette smoke contains roughly 4,000 chemicals. Of these, 200 are poisons. These chemicals and poisons can cause a variety of health problems, including bad breath, loss of smell and taste, and stained teeth and fingers. Cigarettes are also known to cause many deadly health conditions, such as **emphysema**, high **blood pressure**, stroke, heart disease, and cancer.

Smoking causes hundreds of thousands of deaths in the United States every year. Once a person begins smoking, it is very difficult to stop. Cigarettes can become an addiction. This means the body starts to depend on the chemicals in the cigarettes. Some studies show that one out of every three young people who experiment with smoking is addicted by the age of 20.

Alcohol can be as dangerous as smoking. It goes straight from the stomach into the bloodstream. Blood carries it to other parts of the body. When alcohol reaches the brain, it can affect how a person thinks and acts. The liver is the organ that rids the body of alcohol. Alcohol abuse can cause damage to the liver, heart, and nervous system, as well as loss of memory, low vitamin levels, and changes in a person's behavior.

Healthy Lung

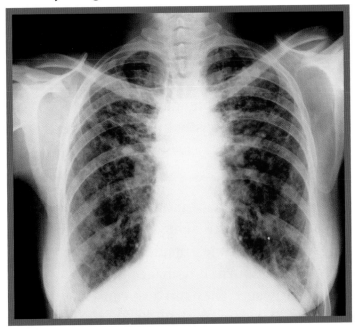

Smoker's Lung

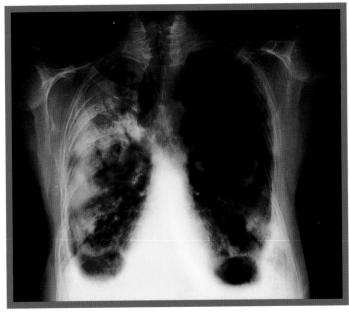

⌃ Using special tools such as X-rays or CT scans, doctors can see a person's lungs. Healthy lungs appear clear. Damaged lungs appear red, brown, and black.

Digging Deeper

Your Challenge!

Many of the chemicals found in cigarettes are used in other ways. Some are used in cleaning products, while others are used to pave roads. Research in the library and online to find the names of as many cigarette chemicals as you can. Then, learn more about each chemical to discover any other ways it may be used. The results may surprise you!

Summary

Behaviors such as smoking and consuming alcohol can be harmful to your health, and sometimes deadly.

Further Inquiry

Besides dangerous chemicals, things that seem harmless can be bad for our bodies, too. Sunshine, for example, can harm the skin. Maybe we should ask,

Why is too much sunshine dangerous to health?

Why Is Too Much Sunshine Dangerous to Health?

Most people enjoy spending time outside on sunny days. Beaches are often crowded in the summer with people trying to get a suntan. Although sunlight is pleasant and supplies energy for much of the life on Earth, it can do great harm to people.

Sunshine contains ultraviolet (UV) rays. People cannot see these rays, but they can harm the body by causing sunburns. They are especially dangerous if a person spends a great deal of time outside without protection. Every time a person gets a sunburn, it damages the skin. Sunburns can cause wrinkles at an early age. They can also cause skin cancer. Every year in the United States, more than 60,000 people develop skin cancer from Sun exposure.

It is important to protect the body from the Sun's harmful rays. Wear clothing that covers as much skin as possible. Sunscreen is a chemical that prevents UV rays from reaching the skin. Cover exposed skin with sunscreen that has a Sun protection factor (SPF) of at least 15.

❮ Experts recommend that people apply about one ounce of sunscreen 30 minutes before spending time in the sunshine.

Digging Deeper

Your Challenge!

Test how the Sun can cause damage. Take a piece of black construction paper and fold it in half. Apply sunscreen to one half but not the other. Leave the paper in direct sunlight for a few hours. What happened to the construction paper? Is one side darker than the other? In only a few short hours, the Sun faded the paper that was not protected by sunscreen.

Summary

Too much Sun exposure can be harmful. Sunburns damage the skin and may lead to skin cancer.

Further Inquiry

Sometimes, thinking about our health too much can be harmful. Maybe we should ask,

How do thoughts and feelings affect health?

⌃ People who live in tropical areas have higher skin cancer rates than people who live in other parts of the world.

How Do Thoughts and Feelings Affect Health?

The mind and body are connected. This is clear when people are under a great deal of mental stress. Mental stress is the feeling some people get when they take a test or perform in front of an audience. It may feel like they have butterflies in their stomachs.

A problem can occur if people worry about something too much. They may become sick. The reason for this is the chemical cortisol. When under stress, the body will produce cortisol. Cortisol helps the body deal with stressful situations. This chemical, however, is not meant to be in the body for long periods of time. If a person is stressed for a long period of time, the cortisol can build up in the body and cause health problems. These health problems can include depression, slower brain activity, and even heart attacks.

Sometimes, mental stress can be a good thing. For example, it can help people focus on a job to help them do it well. This is when cortisol helps the body, but only for short periods of time. In general, however, stress should be avoided. Positive thoughts and feelings have a much better effect on health. Happy people may be healthier and live longer than unhappy people. Love and friendship can be important. People who are surrounded by good friends, a loving family, and pets may be healthier than lonely people.

> Exercising, taking deep breaths, and finding a quiet place to sit or lie down are just a few ways to relieve stress.

Digging Deeper

Your Challenge!

Understanding how you feel is important to your health. Chart how you feel for one week. Use a series of smiley faces to show how you are feeling. Draw a face with a frown for sad days and faces with smiles for happy days. Write down what made you happy and what made you sad. Then, calculate if you feel happy or sad more. What can you do to have more happy days?

Summary

Being happy is part of having good health. Sometimes, people worry or feel stress. This can impact one's health.

Further Inquiry

Understanding what makes good health has involved asking many questions. Maybe we are ready to put it all together and answer the question,

What is good health?

Putting It All Together

Many factors play a role in good health. What people eat, how much they exercise, what they put into their bodies, and how they protect their bodies are all important. Diseases and sickness happen. When people do get sick, their bodies have natural defense systems. The immune system, including the skin and mucus in the nose and throat, helps protect the body from germs. When germs do enter the body, the defense system attacks and kills the germs. The body regulates itself to keep its internal systems working properly. Medicine can help people overcome illness, but people's actions are also important. Keeping the body safe and putting the best things into its systems will help keep people healthy. Mental health is also important. It is important to learn ways to reduce stress and to worry less. By keeping their minds free from worry and stress, people can keep their bodies healthy.

Where People Fit In

People have an important interest in staying healthy. The decisions people make each day determine whether they will maintain their health. If they are not healthy, they will often get sick and may even die. A diet that includes fresh fruits and vegetables and fewer fatty foods can help people live longer. Exercise is also very important. Good personal hygiene and taking care of one's body are other steps people can take to maintain their health.

❯ Some people join gyms or take exercise classes to stay healthy and reduce stress.

Careers in Health

Doctor

A family doctor is the first health care professional most people see when they have a medical problem. The doctor must talk to and examine the patient, looking for clues as to what is wrong. Once the problem is identified, the doctor suggests a treatment that will help the patient recover. Family doctors treat patients of all ages. Doctors go to medical school and train in clinics and hospitals. They gain experience treating many different illnesses.

Physical Therapist

Physical therapists help people recover from injury, illness, or disability. They create training programs for people who have trouble moving and functioning properly. Massage and developing exercise programs are some of the ways that physical therapists help improve people's health. To become a physical therapist, a person must first complete a master's degree from a university. Then, the person might begin training in an office, or continue their education to specialize in a certain area, such as sports injuries, head and spinal cord injuries, or working with children.

Young Scientists at Work

You can answer the questions below using only the book, your own experiences, and your common sense.

Fact:

Your heart is made of a type of muscle that can work for longer periods of time than the other muscles in your body.

Test:

You will need a watch or clock with a second hand to do this experiment. Make a tight fist with your hand, then relax your hand. Repeat this tightening and relaxing movement 70 times per minute. This is how many times your heart beats every minute.

Predict:

What will happen to the muscles in your hand after performing this test over a short period of time? Your heart does not become tired the way your hand does because it is made of a different type of muscle.

Fact:
Your body has many built-in defenses against germs.

Test:
Which of the following are defenses against germs?

bad breath	earwax
stomach acid	a sneeze
smelly feet	tears
sweat	antibodies

Answers:

Earwax, stomach acid, a sneeze, tears, and antibodies are defenses against germs. Bad breath, smelly feet, and sweat are not.

Take a Health Survey

Answer the questions about smoking. Then, research the effects of smoking at the library and on the Internet to learn more.

1. Are you a smoker, or have you ever tried smoking a cigarette?

2. Have most people your age tried cigarettes?

3. Will it be okay to smoke cigarettes when you are in high school?

4. Is there a relationship between teenage smoking, drinking, and drug abuse?

5. Do most adults smoke cigarettes?

Statistics

Everyday, about 4,000 children in the United States try their first cigarette. About 1,000 of these kids become addicted, daily smokers. Cigarettes contain a very addictive drug called nicotine. A person can become addicted to nicotine in just a few days.

According to a study by the University of Michigan, 8.7 percent of eighth graders and 14.5 percent of tenth graders are smokers. About 21.6 percent of students are smokers by the time they leave high school. About 30 percent of young smokers will die early from smoking related causes.

The U.S. Department of Health and Human Services says that teens between 12 and 17 years of age who smoke are 11 percent more likely to use illegal drugs and 16 percent more likely to drink heavily than those who do not smoke. About 20 percent of adults, or about 45 million people, in the United States smoke.

Key Words

allergies: the immune system's reaction to a substance in the body that causes symptoms such as sneezing, itching, and hives

arthritis: an autoimmune disease that attacks body tissue in joints

arteries: tubes that carry blood from the heart to the rest of the body

asthma: a medical condition that makes it difficult for a person to breathe

blood pressure: the force of blood against the arteries through which it flows

calcium: a mineral that keeps bones and teeth healthy

cells: the basic building blocks of all living material

contagious: describes a disease that can be passed to other people by contact

emphysema: an illness of the lungs that makes breathing difficult and may affect the heart

environment: the conditions or place in which people, animals, and plants live

germs: tiny organisms that cause disease

glands: organs that produce and release substances needed by the body

heart attack: a medical condition in which parts of the heart become damaged or die due to lack of oxygen

homeostasis: the body's tendency to maintain a consistent environment

immune system: the network of cells and tissues that protect the body from harmful organisms

minerals: substances that are important for good health

nutrients: substances that help build tissue and give energy to the body

oxygenated: enriched, or combined, with oxygen

spinal cord: the large bundle of nerves inside the spine

vaccine: medicine that prevents disease

vitamins: natural substances found in food that contribute to good health

Index

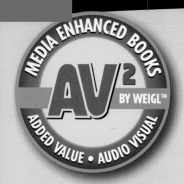

Log on to www.av2books.com

AV² by Weigl brings you media enhanced books that support active learning. Go to www.av2books.com, and enter the special code found on page 2 of this book. You will gain access to enriched and enhanced content that supplements and complements this book. Content includes video, audio, weblinks, quizzes, a slide show, and activities.

AV² Online Navigation

Audio
Listen to sections of the book read aloud.

Book Pages
AV² pages directly correspond to pages in the book.

Video
Watch informative video clips.

Key Words
Study vocabulary, and complete a matching word activity.

Embedded Weblinks
Gain additional information for research.

Quizzes
Test your knowledge.

Slide Show
View images and captions, and prepare a presentation.

Try This!
Complete activities and hands-on experiments.

AV² was built to bridge the gap between print and digital. We encourage you to tell us what you like and what you want to see in the future.

Sign up to be an AV² Ambassador at www.av2books.com/ambassador.